Conducting Meetings

A GUIDE TO RUNNING PRODUCTIVE COMMUNITY ASSOCIATION BOARD MEETINGS

Second Edition

Community Associations Press®
Alexandria, VA

ISBN 978-159618-003-1
© 2005 Community Associations Press®, a division of Community Associations Institute.

Community Associations Press
A Division of Community Associations Institute
225 Reinekers Lane, Ste. 300
Alexandria, VA 22314

To order additional copies of this book, please write to the publisher at the address above or call (703) 548-8600. You can also order online at *www.caionline.org/bookstore.cfm*.

This publication is designed to provide accurate and authoritative information in regard to the subject matter covered. It is sold with the understanding that the publisher is not engaged in rendering legal, accounting, or other professional services. If legal advice or other expert assistance is required, the services of a competent professional should be sought.
—From a Declaration of Principles, jointly adopted by a Committee of the American Bar Association and a Committee of Publishers

Printed in the United States of America

Library of Congress Cataloging in Publication Data

    Conducting meetings : a guide to running productive community association board meetings.—
      2nd ed.
      p. cm.
    ISBN-13: 978-1-59618-003-1
    1. Condominium associations—United States—Management. 2. Homeowners' associations—United States—Management. 3. Housing management—United States.
    HD7287.67.U5C653 2006

2005035084

Contents

Acknowledgments

CONTRIBUTORS
Gurdon Buck, ESQ.

Kenneth Budd

Harold Corbin

Raymond Diaz, ESQ.

Christopher Durso

Henry Goodman, ESQ.

Alicia Granados, CMCA, AMS, PCAM

MJ Keatts

Richard Lievens, ESQ.

Peter Philbin, ESQ.

Jim Slaughter

Lucia Anna Trigiani, ESQ.

Pamela Washburn, CMCA, AMS

EDITOR
MJ Keatts

EDITOR, 2ND EDITION
Debra H. Lewin

DESIGNER
Cori Canady

Community Associations Press, the publishing division of Community Associations Institute (CAI), is dedicated solely to publishing the very best resources available for community associations. It publishes the largest collection of books and guides on community associations available today.

Founded in 1973 as a multidisciplinary, nonprofit alliance serving all stakeholders in community associations, CAI is the only national organization dedicated to fostering vibrant, responsive, competent community associations. Our mission is to assist community associations in promoting harmony, community, and responsible leadership.

CAI has more than 26,000 members in more than 55 chapters throughout the United States. To find out more about CAI, visit www.caionline.org or call CAI Direct at (703) 548-8600 or (888) 224-4321 (Mon–Fri, 9:00–6:30 ET).

Introduction

It's the monthly board meeting, and you're meeting in the kitchen of the president's home. The first item on the agenda? Chaos. As the secretary reviews the minutes, Little Jimmy, the president's three-year-old son, bangs a drum and parades around the table. Older son Joey fights with his sister over the television, which is only slightly louder than an Apollo moon launch. Freida, the treasurer, continually leaves the table to grab doughnuts, while Fred, a homeowner whose voice is actually louder than the TV, lobbies for approval of his Brady Bunch garden gnomes. With each interruption, the discussion strays to new and unrelated topics—when Freida explains the relationship between pet problems and UFO abductions, the president searches for the agenda, which, unfortunately, was eaten by the dog. Finally, after four hours and 16 minutes, the meeting adjourns, due to a lack of additional doughnuts.

This is not the way to hold a board meeting.

A board meeting is not a social gathering. It isn't a time to gossip, socialize, or promote a personal agenda. It's a business meeting. And if your board meetings are lasting longer than two hours—with little accomplished—then something is wrong. Maybe it's the venue. Maybe it's disorganization. Maybe it's lack of leadership.

Unproductive meetings create unproductive boards. They increase frustration, destroy morale, and make it harder to recruit volunteers. They also waste everyone's time.

A compilation of previously published *Common Ground* and *Community Management* articles, this book helps community association directors and managers organize and orchestrate effective, efficient board meetings. It also discusses how to take proper meeting minutes, the potential benefits and drawbacks of recording meetings, and appropriate agenda items for executive sessions.

Productive board meetings are the foundation of a successful community association; by taking the right steps, directors and managers will be able to conduct them effectively.

CHAPTER 1

Proper Meeting Preparation

BY KENNETH BUDD AND MJ KEATTS

Advance Planning Boosts Board Productivity

Meetings at Shelter Creek, a 1,296-unit community in San Bruno, California, used to last three to four hours. Now they last no more than two hours. Mike Yarman, AMS, Shelter Creek's manager, attributes the improvement to advance planning. He meets with the president the night before the meeting to discuss the agenda. If the agenda is particularly full, he holds a 45-minute study session two weeks before the meeting.

Study Sessions

The study session is an open forum for directors and members. For example, if the association was scheduled to decide on an insurance contract at its next meeting, insurance representatives would be invited to the study sessions to answer questions.

"Board members get more out of it than if they just received a meeting packet," Yarman said. "They come to the meeting prepared."

Board Meeting Packets

Rob Felix, CMCA, PCAM, manager of the Sun City Vistoso Community Association in Tucson, Arizona, agrees. Felix distributes information packets to each board member one week before the meeting. The packets include copies of the meeting agenda, treasurer's report, committee reports, management report, minutes from the last board meeting, and any pertinent correspondence or documents. By giving board members a chance to review the agenda before the meeting, Felix can answer their questions and is able to anticipate potential problems.

Felix discusses the agenda with the president before the meeting and offers advice on the issues at hand. After he meets with the president, he knows if he needs to collect more information.

Bill Overton, PCAM, manager of the Wailea Community Association in Maui, Hawaii, also distributes information packets to each board member before the meeting. In addition to discussing the agenda with the president, he summarizes the association's business and his recommendations in a cover letter, which he inserts in the front of the board members' information packets.

"I use the cover letter to present my recommendations to the board in writing," Overton said. "Sometimes board members respond better to a recommendation when it's presented in writing than when it's presented orally. If a manager seems pushy in a meeting, the board reacts negatively."

Managers will know they have adequately prepared for a board meeting when they do not need to interact very much during the meeting. "The board will be ready to govern and won't require any additional information," Overton said.

Like Preparing for Court

"Preparing for a board meeting is like preparing for court," said Linnea Juarez, PCAM, president of Condominium Financial Management, Inc. in Martinez, California. "Managers must have their arguments laid out and anticipate [board members'] cross examination."

Juarez, who teaches managers how to effectively organize and facilitate board meetings, once observed a board meeting where the manager presented three bids for a fence repair. "Didn't we have this fence fixed two years ago?" a board member asked the manager. "Who fixed it then?" The manager didn't know.

"The manager should have collected this information before the meeting," Juarez said. "He didn't do his homework."

Strict Agendas Maintain Structure

Regardless of how well a manager prepares for a meeting, there is always the chance that a rambling speaker could jeopardize the board's productivity. Agendas with time limits, however, enable the president to effectively guide meeting discussions.

Joseph Carleton, Jr., a Maine attorney and legislator, says an agenda with start times and time limits gives the meeting structure.

"They make directors more aware of time," Carleton said. "They

Board meetings are the foundation of an association's business operations.

provide a subtle reminder if you're falling behind in the discussion." Carleton also suggests that the president remind directors of time limits before the meeting begins.

When a board is expecting a large, demanding audience —perhaps due to a large special assessment or an unattended maintenance problem—it may consider beginning its agenda by allowing 20–30 minutes for comments from the crowd. If owners are still asking questions after 30 minutes, the board president should announce that he or she will take three more questions. This strategy lets owners know that their time is up, but keeps them from feeling cut off by the president.

Board meetings are the foundation of an association's business operations. Come prepared to make important decisions. And let a detailed agenda be your guide. When the meeting adjourns, directors will leave knowing they efficiently and effectively performed their fiduciary duties. ∎

BY PAM WASHBURN, CMCA, AMS

Board Packets Reduce Meeting Times

Do your board meetings last for hours? If so, it could be because your board members aren't prepared. And if they're not prepared, they're probably not receiving a board packet (or they're receiving a packet so unorganized that it's impossible to comprehend).

Managers should prepare and distribute board packets 10 days before each board meeting. The packet should include minutes from the previous meeting; finance, committee, management, and treasurer's reports; correspondence; and, most importantly, the meeting agenda. Preparing the packet will take time, but it will ultimately save time. It will lead to better informed, better prepared boards, and smoother, more efficient meetings.

Effective Agendas

An effective agenda is the backbone of the board packet. The agenda should include enough details to help board members prepare for the meeting. Simply stating "Treasurer's Report" or "New Business" isn't enough. Under each agenda heading, list the main points that will be discussed. An example might be:

NEW BUSINESS: (10:50 A.M.)

A. Recommendation to approve Exterior Change Request No. 8279 to install plantings on the common grounds at the rear of the lot line.

B. Recommendations from the Safety and Security Committee to make improvements to the entrance security systems.

C. Discussion on issues regarding upcoming budget preparation.

- Board's opinions regarding user fee increases.
- Board's priorities for capital acquisitions.
- Management's projections regarding annual costs to operate new Pitch and Putt golf course.

Also include benchmark times on the agenda. For example, "Call to Order—10:00 a.m.," "Approval of Minutes—10:05." This lets board members know how time will be allotted and keeps the meeting moving. At my association, we typically schedule two-hour board meetings. The agendas also include the times and dates of future board meetings, workshops, and events, to further allow directors to plan.

Organizing the Packet

The meeting packet should be prepared in the same chronological order as the agenda. Use colored paper or tabs to mark the beginning of different sections. Label each item to correspond with the agenda. You can also design a form to serve as the cover sheet for each packet item. The form should contain brief background facts, committee recommendations if applicable, and management's recommendations.

If you do not use a form, be sure to include your recommendations on key agenda items with your monthly manager's report. Board meetings are not the place to tell directors how you feel. Prepare them ahead of time.

The packet material should be concise and complete. I find it helpful to prepare the agenda throughout the month, and make copies of the packet items as time permits. However you do it, board packets work. They enable your board members to arrive at meetings prepared to take action. The board at my association consistently completes the agenda—without spending hours in the meeting. ∎

BY KENNETH BUDD

Boards Can't Conduct Business in the Kitchen

When board members began bringing food scraps to meetings, Judy Burd, CMCA, AMS, PCAM, knew there was a problem. Actually, there were two problems: two fluffy little dogs named Yip and Yap, as Burd, of Legum & Norman, Inc. in McLean, Virginia, liked to call them.

Yip and Yap belonged to a board member who brought them to every meeting. The dogs would scamper about the room, yipping and yapping. Directors brought the food scraps to keep the dogs quiet. At the end of the director's term, she moved to a neighboring building. Her reputation preceded her. When Yip and Yap moved in, the board of directors passed a rule stating that "no pets are permitted to attend meetings of the association."

Eliminating distractions is essential for running a meeting. Would IBM hold an important board meeting with dogs scurrying around the room? Hopefully not.

The Business Venue

IBM also wouldn't hold a meeting in the CEO's kitchen. Meetings should be held in an environment that enhances productivity. A meeting in a board member's home will typically invite more distractions, from pets to the television. Consider more formal settings—if the association has a clubhouse, find an available room. If the manager has an office, hold the meeting there. Many public libraries have meeting rooms available for minimal fees.

"It helps maintain a business-like atmosphere," said Joseph Carleton, Jr., a Maine attorney and legislator.

Some meeting experts believe a business-like setting does not include food. Food can be disruptive—imagine directors munching on corn chips during the management report. According to Carleton, refreshments are fine for the beginning of the meeting, or at a break in the middle, but not during the meeting. Some

Encouraging Board Members to Show

Directors who perpetually arrive late to meetings—or who don't show at all—can stifle a board's productivity. Here are some common reasons for board member tardiness and absenteeism and some ways to prevent such habits from jeopardizing board effectiveness:

Plausible Reasons
- Most board members juggle family, business, and community responsibilities.
- Some associations hold board meetings too frequently.
- Meetings exceed two hours and are perceived as unproductive.
- Association bylaws lack clearly defined board member roles and responsibilities.
- Association bylaws lack penalties for failure to attend board meetings.
- Some boards provide insufficient notice of schedule changes.

Possible Solutions
- Explain the importance of attending meetings to current and incoming board members; ask frequent absentees if they really want to continue serving on the board.
- Amend association bylaws to mandate dismissal from the board after two consecutive unexcused absences.
- Survey members at each meeting—and follow-up with absent members—to learn the best time for the next meeting.
- Institute a buddy system to keep members informed when they miss a meeting.

Source: Development and Technical Assistance Center in New Haven, Connecticut

associations, however, serve cookies, sodas, and coffee during their meetings—they feel it creates a nicer atmosphere.

One thing that does not create a nicer atmosphere, Burd said, is smoking. She believes cigarettes are distracting—her board meetings are strictly nonsmoking. Board meetings are business meetings, not poker games. Alcohol is even worse than cigarettes. It affects decision making, and an empty wine bottle usually corresponds with diminished productivity.

"I don't like the connotations of having alcohol at a meeting," Burd said. "If there is a controversial decision, or if a director seems out of control, residents could later say the director was drunk."

Day Break or Nightfall

When is the best time of day to hold meetings? It depends on the personalities and time constraints of the board members. What works for one board may not work for another.

There are pros and cons for various times. David Gibbons, CMCA, PCAM, CPM of Quadrant, Inc. in Myrtle Beach, South Carolina, is a proponent of day meetings. Gibbons believes directors need to be at their top mental and physical condition when meeting. That's difficult after working an eight-hour day, fighting through rush hour traffic, and wolfing down a quick meal and a cocktail (or after no meal at all). Gibbons thinks directors should meet early, at 7:00 or 7:30 a.m., before heading to work. This inspires them to hold quicker, more efficient meetings. Another alternative is to hold the meeting at 4:00 or 4:30 in the afternoon, rather than late in the evening.

Others argue that day meetings are unrealistic and more likely to exclude homeowners who work. So what's the best evening time? Mike Yarman, AMS, has found that the last Wednesday of the month at 7:00 p.m. works best for both board members and homeowners at Shelter Creek in San Bruno, California. Rather than stressing out directors, Yarman thinks the 7:00 p.m. start time gives them time to get home from work, unwind, and have dinner before attending the meeting. Others suggest 7:30 p.m.

No More Than Two Hours

While there is no consensus on when to hold a meeting, most experts agree that meetings should not last more than two hours.

"Most people become unproductive after an hour-and-a half," Carleton said. "At that point, it may be more productive to continue at another time." As Gibbons noted, when tired, frustrated people make rash, last-second decisions, the result can be an even longer meeting filled with hundreds of angry owners. ∎

CHAPTER 2

Staying on Course

BY KENNETH BUDD

Keeping the Meeting Moving

Writing an agenda and preparing board packets does not guarantee an effective meeting. Boards can still stray from the agenda, which adds countless minutes to the meeting—a discussion on pool contracts leads to a discussion on pool halls, which results in a 15-minute debate on The Music Man. Keeping the discussion focused on association business is the responsibility of the meeting chair—typically, the president.

The Enforcer

"The president determines the flow of business," said Joseph Carleton, Jr., a Maine attorney and legislator. "He or she keeps the others in check and suggests when it's time to stop talking and start voting." The president, Carleton said, is the mediator—the guiding force who prevents 30-minute monologues and gossip sessions, and searches for consensus in the group. When the discussion deteriorates or heads in another direction, the president needs to steer it back. The manager can also help keep the meeting on track.

Include a Solution

As part of the steering process, Brent Herrington, PCAM, manager of Disney's Celebration in Florida, has another suggestion: never present an issue—particularly a minor one—without a proposed solution.

"Any time you dangle a topic in front of a group of people and invite them to opine about it, everyone will feel challenged to weigh-in with some insightful observations and off-the-cuff opinions," said Herrington, in a message posted on CAI's website. Instead, Herrington recommends that the manager, the president, or a committee research issues before the meeting and propose solutions.

For example, if a resident inquires about extending the pool hours, the president or manager can say: "For the next item on the agenda, I recommend we revise our pool rules so the facility can remain open until 10:00 p.m. during the months of June, July, and August. This is in response to a member request. I have weighed the pros and cons and believe it will be a positive change for the community. Assuming the board is supportive, I would like to announce this change in the May newsletter, with the condition that the change is on a trial basis and will be reevaluated in July. Is there a motion to approve my recommendation?"

You may have just saved 30 minutes.

Making Decisions

Meetings are for making decisions. A board meeting is not the time to begin the decision-making process or discuss minor issues.

"The board shouldn't have to discuss late fees—the manager should handle that," said Linda Farsi, CMCA, PCAM, vice president of Community Group in Virginia Beach, Virginia. Farsi wrote about meetings for CAI's Southeastern Virginia Chapter. "Meetings shouldn't be an occasion to micromanage the manager. The board should be making decisions about important issues, like contracts and large expenditures."

Diffusing Meeting Conflicts

Conflicts can come to a head in board meetings, particularly when directors feel shut out of the decision-making process. Excluded from the debate, that person sits and stews, until he or she becomes hostile. How can you prevent that anger from building? By giving each director a chance to contribute.

Sam Dolnick, former president of the Lake Park Condominium Association in La Mesa, California, said his association posts its agendas 14 days before a meeting. Members of the board can add or remove topics within seven days, at which point the final agenda is posted. At the meeting, the president will ask if an emergency has arisen that should be added to the agenda. This gives everyone at least two opportunities to add items to the agenda.

Equal Time and Courtesy

This is only the first step, however. Once the meeting starts, each director—not one dominant personality—needs time to express his or her views.

"Sometimes personality conflicts arise because of insensitivity," said Ellen Hirsch de Haan, an attorney with Becker & Poliakoff in

Votes don't change things—they validate them. It's the discussion that matters.

St. Petersburg, Florida. "One of the best ways to defuse a potentially volatile situation is to give a person time to talk. Courtesy can make a difference."

Courtesy also means that everyone speaks for the same amount of time. Boards may want to write regulations for this—for example, each person can speak for three minutes, and can't speak again until everyone has spoken. Such a procedure ensures fairness and prevents frustration from building in less vocal directors. Otherwise, Dolnick said, some people will speak more than others, and the president could be accused of favoritism.

Equal Protection

Equal time, however, should be matched by equal protection—specifically protection from personal attacks.

"When anyone makes a personal attack, the gavel goes down," Dolnick said. "That's out of order. It's healthy to argue, but I don't consider arguing to be conflict. Conflict is name calling and interrupting. It's destructive."

Finally, if meetings are constantly plagued by "demagogue" owners determined to "divide and conquer" board unity, consider asking an off-duty, uniformed police officer to observe the meeting. Though the officer will have no power at the meeting, most attendees will respond with respect.

Parliamentary Procedure

A structured meeting—one that follows *Robert's Rules of Order* or some form of parliamentary procedure—also can help control conflicts. But those procedures should be consistent. Directors should not cite obscure technicalities from *Robert's Rules* if the board doesn't normally use them. That in itself will create conflict, not control. Sam Gladding, a professor at Wake Forest University who specializes in counseling and group work, believes boards shouldn't feel compelled to use *Robert's Rules* if it is causing frustration.

Organized Discussion

"It isn't the only way to run a group," Gladding said. "*Robert's Rules* tend to make a group more stiff and formal. Many times it inhibits real conversation rather than facilitating it." Organized discussion, Gladding believes, is the critical component in making decisions and casting votes that don't destroy a group. Voting can create winners and losers. For the losers, Gladding said, the result can be either great apathy or great hostility. Forcing a decision down others' throats and not building some form of consensus is a recipe for conflict. According to Robert Dennistoun, author of *The Board President*, ideas need to be explained, not proclaimed.

"If the goal is to advance an idea and to convince people of it, you need to do your homework and discuss it," Dennistoun said. "Votes don't change things—they validate them. It's the discussion that matters." ∎

BY HAROLD CORBIN

Parliamentarians Offer Guidance on Meeting Procedures

An association board meeting is the place for members to resolve old business and discuss new plans. But unless meetings are run in a well-organized manner, chaos can, and frequently does, reign. To ensure that everyone has a fair hearing, that members' rights are protected, and that the meeting's objectives are met, the association needs to follow parliamentary procedure.

Some associations have members who are well-versed in the intricacies of parliamentary procedure. But other associations may need to employ a professional parliamentarian.

The Parliamentarian

The parliamentarian must be familiar with the association's bylaws, rules and procedures, and the minutes of the last meeting. Also, the parliamentarian must be familiar with the agenda, ensure that it's followed, and that questions are handled appropriately.

It's not the parliamentarian's job to control the meeting, but to advise and maintain order. He or she may offer advice when questioned or speak to the members and explain opinions.

A Sound Investment

A parliamentarian's fee should be based on the amount of time he or she spends preparing for and attending the board meeting. Generally, the association also pays for the parliamentarian's travel expenses.

Hiring a parliamentarian to attend board meetings is a sound investment. A parliamentarian who is impartial, consistent, and tactful is invaluable to the presiding officer and the entire association. ∎

Don't Be Afraid of Parliamentary Procedure

Parliamentary procedure is vital for a smooth-running meeting. But *Robert's Rules of Order*—the bible of parliamentary procedure—can be difficult to understand. Fortunately, there are some basic rules of parliamentary procedure that can be easily followed by all associations. They include:

- Follow the agenda
- Discuss one subject at a time
- Give each board member a chance to speak
- Speak only on the issue being discussed
- Speak only when recognized by the chair
- Address questions and comments to the chair
- Decide issues through motions, seconds, and votes

BY JIM SLAUGHTER

Motions Made Simple

The key to parliamentary procedure is the motion. While there are a lot of them—*Robert's Rules* lists more than 80 in its central table—most meetings stick to about a dozen. Not all motions are in order at any given moment. Instead, certain motions are considered ahead of others in formal procedure. This concept is known as "precedence." The commonly used motions listed below are in order of precedence, from lowest- to highest-ranking motion.

- Main motion: brings business before the assembly; permitted only when no other motion is pending.
- Amendment: allows modifications to another motion by adding, deleting, or changing words.
- Refer: allows a matter to be sent to a smaller group to consider and report back.
- Postpone: delays consideration of a matter.
- Limit debate: places a limit on the time or number of speakers.
- Previous question: ends debate immediately.
- Table: temporarily delays a matter when something urgent arises.
- Recess: permits a short break.
- Adjourn: ends the meeting.

Precedence is governed by two rules: 1. When a motion is being considered, any motion higher on the list may be proposed. 2. The motion last proposed (and highest on the list) is considered and decided first.

Example

Main motion: The main motion being discussed is to authorize $5,000 for painting.

Amendment: A motion is made to amend the main motion by striking "$5,000" and inserting "$7,500," which is in order, as it's higher on the list than the main motion.

Refer: During discussion of the amendment, a motion is made to refer the matter to a committee, which is also in order.

Postpone: During discussion on the motion to refer, a motion is made to postpone the matter until next month's meeting—again, in order.

Adjourn: A member then moves to adjourn the entire meeting, also in order.

Recess: Prior to voting on the motion to adjourn, a member obtains the floor and moves to recess for five minutes. The motion to recess is out of order because it is lower on the list than the motion to adjourn.

This may seem like an unnecessarily elaborate process for what seems like a simple item of business. But the assembly had only one question before it at any given moment, and members focused on the immediately pending motion only and avoided distractions.

Other commonly used motions include:

- Point of order: calls attention to an error in procedure.
- Point of information: allows a member to ask a question.
- Division of the assembly: demands a rising (but not counted) vote after a voice vote.

BY PETER PHILBIN, ESQ.

Swatting at Gadflies

The meeting is going well, when suddenly there is a disturbing buzzing noise. Flying dangerously around the room is an angry, insect-like creature, and it is blaming the association for everything from an assessment increase to the divorce of Michael and Lisa Marie. It's the dreaded gadfly.

Just about anyone involved with community associations has encountered the gadfly. It's an expert at criticizing, cajoling, and pinpointing the errors of others—even when these errors don't exist.

The gadfly demands change, but rarely devotes the time or effort needed to create positive change. It may mean well, but it never channels those good intentions into constructive efforts.

The gadfly often emerges at association meetings and creates an atmosphere of chaos and paralysis. The gadfly raises parliamentary issues, alleges noncompliance with statutory or governing document provisions, and constantly interrupts. It attacks board members' personal integrity and alleges conflicts of interest.

Gadflies Aren't Dissenters

Dissent can be healthy and productive and is an essential part of the democratic process. But gadflies and dissenters are two different creatures.

Dissenters may disagree with an approach, but they offer alternatives and work within the established rules to accomplish their goals. Gadflies ignore rules of order, are rude, disregard the process, and only appear satisfied when their demands are met. Some associations create gadflies by not keeping their members informed. Some members, however, are born gadflies—and even one gadfly can infect a meeting with confusion.

What can the board or manager do to maintain order?

It's Not a Homeowner Meeting

When dealing with a gadfly in a board meeting, remember that these are not homeowner meetings. The meeting is for the board to conduct the business of the association.

While community associations should open their meetings and generally are required to by law, this does not mean that owners are entitled to participate uncontrollably. There are several ways to deal with the gadfly in this setting:

Announce Meeting Procedures

Sometimes owners who attend board meetings are not familiar with meeting procedure. At the beginning of the meeting, the presiding officer should explain the meeting process and state when the board will accept comments from homeowners. If the presiding officer announces that the board will not allow home-owner comments, then it must follow this policy consistently—not just with the gadfly.

It's sometimes difficult to enforce a policy limiting home-owner comments—especially when the vast majority of the meeting attendees are prepared to provide constructive suggestions or helpful information. But if the primary goal is to constrain the gadfly, then the board must enforce the restriction uniformly for it to be effective.

Host a Homeowner Forum

Many boards schedule a few minutes before or after the meeting for owners to express their thoughts. The time limit per person may depend on the number of owners at the meeting and the business at hand. Many associations allow each resident three-to-five minutes to speak. But at the end of the allotted time (a total of 20–30 minutes maximum), the board moves on to its planned agenda. Some boards will pass a rule of order requiring owners who wish to speak at the meeting to notify the board or manager in writing. Such a rule helps the board plan its agenda and dis-courages aimless or spontaneous homeowner speeches.

Association documents and state statutes rarely require such a forum; however, it can be an effective way for the board and man-ager to stay in touch with the community and maintain meeting control. A forum also gives the gadfly a chance to "vent" at one specified time—hopefully reducing the gadfly's tendency to inter-rupt throughout the meeting.

By understanding the purpose of the meeting, the rights and obligations of the parties, and parliamentary authority, boards can accomplish... the business of the association.

It's best to hold the homeowner forum before or after the meeting. This way, the gadfly's statements are not part of the official record.

Don't Respond with Anger

The board and manager must not argue or trade insults with the gadfly. Usually it is best to let the gadfly complain for a few minutes during the homeowner forum and then buzz away. Remember, the gadfly is energized by hostility or confrontation. If a response is necessary, the board or manager can wait until after the homeowner forum and "correct" the record. The board does not need to engage the gadfly or give it rebuttal time.

Use Parliamentary Control

The board has a choice: feed the gadfly or clip its wings. It depends on your knowledge of parliamentary tools. This means knowing when and how to 1. table a motion, 2. postpone a motion indefinitely, 3. refer a matter to a committee, 4. adopt special rules of order, and 5. limit debate.

Parliamentary authority was created to bring order to a proceeding. A good working knowledge of parliamentary authority can mean the difference between paralysis and efficiency. If the association's governing documents or state statutes do not specify such authority, the board should adopt a rule of order requiring the use of parliamentary procedure.

Gadflies on the Board

Controlling gadflies who serve on the board is a bit more complex than diffusing gadflies sitting in the audience. If a gadfly is serving on the board, the association could be facing its own form of political gridlock.

In most cases, the homeowner is elected or appointed to the board to fill a vacancy and remains in office until he or she resigns or is removed.

Gadfly board members may harp on pet issues or repeatedly demand the board to review a proposed action. An unprepared board or chair may improperly refuse to recognize motions or allow discussion on the matter. Other chairs will allow the gadfly to drone on until some type of motion is presented and defeated—after a lot of wasted time and energy.

Gadfly Strategy

To prevent this type of paralysis, the chair or president may need to play politician and plan a strategy with other members before the meeting. For example, by anticipating the gadfly's motion, the prepared members can move to postpone it indefinitely. If the motion to postpone indefinitely is adopted, the gadfly's motion is essentially dead unless revived by a motion to reconsider.

Removing the Gadfly

Sometimes the gadfly's actions become too disruptive and the board needs to propose the member's removal—before productive board members resign en masse. The board should carefully consider such a proposal, as the association members will inquire why the gadfly's removal is being sought. Explanations, if any, must be presented clearly and factually supported. While the chance of obtaining enough votes to warrant the gadfly's removal may be small given the governing document's provisions, scheduling the meeting may prompt the gadfly to resign voluntarily.

Board meetings do not need to dissolve into paralysis. By understanding the purpose of the meeting, the rights and obligations of the parties, and parliamentary authority, boards can accomplish what they are supposed to accomplish at their meetings—the business of the association. ∎

Can the Gadfly be Tamed?
By Kenneth Budd

Taming gadflies is difficult, but not impossible. According to James Cachine, AMS, PCAM, of Legum & Norman, Inc. in McLean, Virginia, one trick is to assign the gadfly a special project or appoint it to a committee.

"This can give them a new perspective on the association and encourage them to work with you, instead of against you," said Cachine. "They begin to see things differently."

Another way to tame the gadfly is simply to call its bluff. The late Jerry Fien, a New Jersey homeowner and former *Common Ground* contributing editor, said that if a gadfly begins to complain loudly enough, he will ask them, "What would you recommend?"

"They usually don't have an answer," Fien said.

Cachine adds that since most gadflies rarely want to become involved in the association, asking them to volunteer can be a way to frighten them off. "Once they see that you want them to do some work, they become less involved," he said.

BY JIM SLAUGHTER

Meeting Myth-Understandings

Different chairs running different meetings in different community associations make the same mistakes that are often the result of meeting myths. Things are done a certain way either because "they've always been done that way" or because people believe they're *supposed* to be done that way.

Some rules are made to be broken—especially when they aren't really rules in the first place. In this spirit, what follows are meeting myths that need to be put to rest.

MYTH: **We don't use parliamentary procedure.**

Actually, you do. Whether you're aware of it or not, both your board and annual meetings follow parliamentary procedure. Courts have held that all organizations must observe proper rules when meeting to transact business.

Some associations adopt a rule that they'll follow a particular procedure, such as *Robert's Rules of Order*. Since boards who act contrary to their own rules can be held liable, ignoring or incorrectly applying parliamentary procedure can lead to embarrassment and lawsuits.

MYTH: **Parliamentary procedure and Robert's Rules of Order are the same thing.**

Robert's Rules of Order Newly Revised (Tenth Edition) (RONR) is simply the most popular of several parliamentary books. Another well-known authority is *The Standard Code of Parliamentary Procedure* (Fourth Edition), often referred to simply as *Sturgis*, after its original author, Alice Sturgis.

For the novice, *Sturgis* is a much easier book from which to learn procedure. But the fact that *RONR* is the most-used parliamentary book and the easiest to locate argues in its favor. Just be sure to buy the right book; there are numerous earlier editions that are easy to buy by mistake.

MYTH: **Rules are the same for all meetings.**

The level of procedure usually varies with the size of the assembly. You should keep large annual meetings fairly formal, for example, because informal discussion is impractical due to the number of members present. Plus, formal votes help avoid legal challenges.

In contrast, because formality can hinder business in a meeting of fewer than about a dozen, you can take a lighter approach with smaller boards and committees. Some smaller boards dislike informality and follow a more formal procedure at all meetings—and even informal boards should be more formal on matters of sufficient importance or controversy.

MYTH: **The absence of a quorum is okay if nobody brings it up.**

Not true! A quorum is the number of voting members who must be present to have a valid meeting. This number is typically established by statute or the governing documents. One of the quickest paths to serious trouble is to ignore your quorum requirements. Some state laws allow for a meeting to start with a quorum and to continue after a quorum leaves, but this is very different from not having a quorum in the first place.

MYTH: **Discussion first, motion later.**

If your board is following formal procedure, no discussion should occur without being preceded by a motion to take action. A motion is a formal proposal for consideration and action. In formal meetings, every item of business—whether a proposal to construct a new building or to take a five-minute break—needs a motion.

MYTH: **Seconds are vital.**

While seconds serve a useful purpose, they should not be overemphasized. A second implies that at least one other person wants to discuss a matter. In formal gatherings, such as annual meetings, a second determines whether a proposal will go into discussion. If there is no second, there should be no further action on the proposal.

MYTH: **Vote on all reports.**

Committee reports are often prepared for information purposes only. In such instances, no motion is necessary following the report. A motion to adopt or to accept a report is seldom wise except when the report is to be published in your association's name.

On the other hand, if the committee has a specific recommendation for action, the board would act on it by making a motion.

MYTH: **A motion is always necessary.**

Non-controversial matters can sometimes be resolved without the usual requirement of a motion and vote, through general consent (also known as unanimous consent). Under this method,

What is sometimes misnamed old business is actually unfinished business.

following a motion (or sometimes even without one), the presiding officer asks, for example, "Is there any objection to ending debate?" If no one objects, debate is closed. If a member objects, the matter should be resolved with a motion and vote.

General consent allows you to move quickly through non-controversial issues, adopt reports and motions, approve minutes, and end debate.

MYTH: **The maker of a motion gets to speak first and last.**

The maker of a motion has the right to speak first. After that, the maker has no more rights than anyone else with regard to the motion.

MYTH: **Anyone can speak.**

Meetings are for members. Only board members have a right to participate at board meetings, and only association members have a right to participate at membership meetings. While an assembly can then *permit* anyone to speak, no one but members can demand that right.

MYTH: **A "friendly amendment" is okay.**

Some associations allow any two members to amend a motion on the floor, as long as the change is friendly to the original maker of the motion. Instead of using friendly amendments, the proper practice would be to use unanimous consent ("If there is no objection to this change,...") or to require that the amendment be made formally.

MYTH: **We have "old business."**

What is sometimes misnamed old business is actually unfinished business. Unfinished business refers to questions carried over from the previous meeting and includes:

■ any matter that was pending when the previous meeting adjourned;

■ any matter on the previous meeting's agenda that was not reached; or

■ any matter that was postponed to the present meeting.

MYTH: **Calling "Question!" stops all business.**

The motion to close debate is regularly mishandled. Some believe that stating, "call the question," or simply "Question!" or motioning to close debate automatically ends discussion. Both procedures are wrong. Only the entire assembly decides when to end debate.

The motion to close debate is just another motion, and the maker must be recognized by the chair and have a second. While this motion is not debatable, it does require a two-thirds vote.

MYTH: "Lay on the table" gets rid of sticky issues.

The purpose of the "table" motion is to temporarily delay a matter when something urgent arises. Once the urgent matter is resolved, the group can then resume the matter that was tabled. Because this motion isn't debatable and only requires a majority vote, it can't be used simply to get rid of a matter. In fact, it should be ruled out of order if the evident intent is to avoid dealing with it.

MYTH: The chair runs the meetings.

The chair is the servant of the assembly, not its master. During a meeting, any member can raise a point of order if he or she believes that procedural rules are being violated. This motion can interrupt a speaker and does not require a second. For example:

Member: Point of order!

Chair: What is your point of order?

Member: We are about to move to a new topic, but we haven't voted on the last motion.

The chair rules on the point of order, and any two members can appeal the decision. Thus any question of parliamentary law can be taken from the chair and given to the assembly for decision.

Proper procedure alone won't solve your meeting problems. Burying these myths will bring your meetings more in line and might even make them shorter and more effective. ∎

BY ALICIA GRANADOS, CMCA, AMS, PCAM

Making the Most of Limited Meeting Time

Managers and boards usually only get together once a month. So why waste it? Here are the top five ways managers can help board members make better decisions during limited meeting time.

Think Like a Decision-Maker

Most board members are logical people trying to apply sound business judgment to their decisions. They look to the manager to give them good information. So, before a manager walks into a board meeting, he or she should anticipate what board members may ask about. If there's an item on the agenda about repainting, for example, managers can guess what obvious questions might follow: When was the last time we repainted? How much did it cost? What has our reserve study budgeted for this? Always think in terms of how finances, past experiences, and governing documents might affect an issue.

Be Prepared

The quality—or lack thereof—of a manager's presentation will speak volumes about his or her management skills. For example, a manager might create an overview of the information that's been gathered about a particular issue, and distribute it to board members well in advance of a meeting. A good presentation would also include a summary of relevant provisions from the governing documents or applicable statutes and pertinent financial information, perhaps with critical points highlighted. This gives everyone time to digest information and ask questions in advance, and it demonstrates to the board that they can rely on the manager to cover all bases.

Break It Down

Consider the following classic example of how boards can get sidetracked and waste time. A community originally built with wood-shake shingles has aged to the point where it's facing re-roofing, and the board is drowning in individual requests to change to a different type of shingle. Naturally the board's impulse is to respond to each request. But does it really make sense to debate 50 times about 50 different shingles? No. The goal should be to come up with an unambiguous policy that works for the entire community.

Once the manager helps narrow the focus, he or she can also help break down the task. First, the board should create a committee to identify three or four shingles that fit certain requirements for cost, design, and durability. The next step is to poll the community. Finally, the board can vote on a pre-approved shingle that will replace the wood shakes.

Use a Consent Agenda

Making decisions can be a tough job, but not every issue that a board confronts is monumental. For everyday decisions that don't call for in-depth discussions, use a consent agenda. This is simply a list of items that may be grouped for approval, such as approval of minutes and acceptance of financial statements. By introducing a consent agenda, board members are free to tackle more challenging issues.

Call an Expert

Some issues are beyond the expertise of even the most experienced community manager. Managers should never be afraid to let a board know that they're not experts in every area. Whether it's a legal question or a major engineering project, when the issue at hand exceeds the manager's level of knowledge, it's time to call in an expert.

Managers are exposed to more issues related to community associations in one week than most board members are in an entire year. They should not be afraid to speak up and offer ideas and opinions. With proper preparation and the right attitude, every board meeting provides a chance to build a better relationship. ■

CHAPTER 3

Taking Meeting Minutes

BY GURDON BUCK, ESQ.

Make Meeting Minutes Matter

Meeting minutes are an association's only official record of board decisions and actions. Therefore, it's imperative that these records are taken properly and contain the necessary elements.

The worst basis for a set of good minutes is a bad meeting. If the president or chair fails to follow parliamentary procedure or understand the fundamentals of running a meeting, the resulting minutes will reflect the inevitable chaos.

Meeting minutes reflect what the board decides, not what its members say. If a meeting goes by without a vote or official action being taken, it isn't a meeting, but rather a random gathering of people. Minutes of such a gathering should merely reflect the calling of the opening of the meeting and its adjournment.

The board should have rules of order. They should be included in the association bylaws, or the board can adopt the rules of order at the beginning of each meeting. *Robert's Rules of Order* serves as the standard guide to parliamentary procedure. *The A-B-C's of Parliamentary Procedure* is a simplified version of the information provided in *Robert's Rules of Order*.

The Nature of Minutes

As the name implies, minutes should be brief. Brevity, however, often requires more effort and thought than long-windedness.

It isn't necessary for the secretary to be a member of the board. Some boards hire a professional secretary, an assistant secretary, or a clerk to take the minutes. If the secretary is a director, hiring a minute recorder enables the board secretary to participate in the debate. At a minimum, meeting minutes should contain the following elements:

Type of Meeting

Board meetings are usually described in minutes as regular, special, adjourned regular, or adjourned special meetings.

Association Name
The exact corporate name of the association, and the words "Minutes of the meeting of (name of body)" should be recorded.

Event Information
Specify the meeting date, time, and location.

Attendees' Names
List the names of directors present, the name of the presiding officer, and secretary or substitute minute recorder. For open meetings, the nonvoting audience need not be included. However, if the meeting is a membership meeting, a roll should be taken, and the number of persons or votes present—or at least a quorum—should be announced and entered into the minutes. The roll can be taken at the door by using a name checklist.

Approval of Previous Minutes
Unless the board waives the reading of the minutes, they should be read and approved or corrected. If corrections are necessary, the board should approve the minutes as corrected. Previous meeting minutes are not approved at a special meeting—the minutes should be approved at the next regular meeting. If regular meetings are held less than quarterly, a special committee or the executive committee can be appointed to approve the minutes.

Officer and Committee Reports
Reports made by board and committee members often precede the business of the meeting. Such reports are usually for information only, and if in writing, can be appended to the minutes with board approval. If not in writing, only the fact that the report was made needs to be stated in the minutes. If they contain recommendations for board action, motions to adopt or implement the recommendations should be made by a member other than the reporting officer and acted upon by the board. The board's disposal of the motion may appear in the minutes.

The Business of the Meeting
The minutes should follow the agenda, unless the board agrees to take a matter out of order. The resolutions, exactly as finally made, seconded, and passed, should be grouped according to subject matter. There is no reason to include the summary of

Taking minutes is not equivalent to taking dictation.

debates, discussions, drafts, and revisions of the motions. None of this constitutes official action of the board. The resolution appearing in the minutes should be as voted upon and passed. Reports should be appended to the minutes. The minutes should show each motion as voted upon and whether it was passed, defeated, tabled, returned to committee, etc. In addition, the minutes should include points of order, appeals—whether sustained or lost—and the chair's reason for the ruling.

The resolution should contain a description—including a background statement and introduction—of the matter before the board for discussion and approval. The board will vote on the language of the background statement and resolution. Again, the remarks of individual board members should not be included in the minutes. Members' remarks do not constitute actions of the board, and can lead to future misinterpretations of the board's actions.

In a well-run meeting, the text of the motion will be presented in writing before it is brought to action. If it is included on the meeting agenda, appears in the conclusion of a committee report, or is presented as a written recommendation by the manager, it is more likely that the board will make a sound decision based on revisions and narrowly discussed amendments.

In light of the above reasoning, the motion should be made before the topic is discussed. No motion, no discussion. A discussion without a motion is not only officially out of order, but also creates chaos. A committee report can be made, ending in a motion, if action is required.

Minutes must reflect correct parliamentary procedure. The board should not discuss anything that is not presented in the form of a motion that the board can act upon, or a request for a ruling that the chair can act upon. The only exception to this rule may be a guest speaker. Because the board only recognized the speaker, his or her speech is not the action of the board. In such an instance, only the speaker's name and general topic of the speech should be indicated in the minutes, unless the board moves that the speech be attached to the minutes.

The worst examples of minute taking contain extraneous material. Taking minutes is not equivalent to taking dictation. The secretary's notes should be used as a reference to ensure that motions are worded exactly as passed. If the secretary, or any member of the board, is uncertain about the wording of a motion, it should be reread before final passage.

In a fast-moving meeting, it may be worthwhile to tape the board's actions to ensure that the secretary accurately records the motions. Tape recordings and secretary notes are not official records of the board's actions. Therefore, neither should be available for inspection nor be included in association records. I recommend boards destroy meeting tapes and notes when the minutes are adopted.

A motion is the agreed upon solution to a problem. The actual direction for action by a board should begin with the word "resolved." A motion passed by the board is properly described as a "resolution." The resolution of the problem may have been stated in the background statement and discussed during the debate.

The Vote
If the vote is without objection, the fastest method of passing routine motions, it should be so stated in the minutes. If the vote is by voice, only the chair's ruling needs to be noted by stating "the motion passed." If a board member successfully moves to divide the board by standing, a show of hands, or a paper ballot, the count should be recorded. For small boards, it is proper to show the names of those voting in favor, abstaining, and in opposition to a resolution. Because of a board's fiduciary duty, it is advisable to list those voting with respect to all substantive action motions. It is especially important to list those dissenting, so they are not held responsible for the consequences of an action with which they disagree.

Adjournment
The last paragraph should state the time of adjournment.

Secretary's Signature
The signature of the secretary, preceded by the word "submitted" must be included at the end of the minutes.

Approval at a Subsequent Meeting
The minutes are not official until the board approves them at a subsequent meeting. However, if the subsequent meeting is too far in the future, a committee should be appointed to approve the minutes.

Board meeting minutes are the sole, official reflection of the association's actions. Without them, an association has not acted.

Once approved, they are the official action of the board, regardless of what actually occurred. Thus, by approving the minutes with a differing statement of a resolution, a board can effectively change a passed motion. Minutes can be corrected even after they are approved by a motion to amend (a passed motion) adopted, which requires a two-thirds vote, a majority vote with notice, or a majority of the association members if that is more practical. Minutes cannot be changed to reconsider something that has already been done as a result of the board action, such as issuing a payment or signing a contract agreement.

Inclusion in the Corporate Record Book

The secretary's primary responsibility is maintaining the association's official records. The minute book is the association's principal record. The records should be printed on quality paper, in an official notebook, which should be turned over to the succeeding secretary upon appointment or election to office.

Publication

While publication of minutes is not required, it is recommended for community associations. Minutes should be available for examination by any member upon request.

Board meeting minutes are the sole, official reflection of the association's actions. Without them, an association has not acted. Minutes that reflect board members' remarks and not the board's actions are useless. By including the proper elements in meeting minutes and following parliamentary procedure, association boards will be able to conduct business in an effective and productive manner. ∎

Sample Board Meeting Minutes
By Gurdon Buck, ESQ.

Stonemason Village Condominium Association, Inc.
Minutes of the Meeting of the Executive Board

The regular monthly meeting of the Executive Board of Stonemason Village Condominium Association, Inc. was held on Tuesday, January 19, 2006 at 8:30 p.m. at the clubhouse. The president chaired the meeting and the secretary was present. All members of the board were present. Mr. Hugh L. Dewey, counsel to the association, and Mr. John Handy, association manager, were also present.

The minutes of the last meeting were read and approved as corrected.

The treasurer reported the receipt of an unbudgeted bill from the Acme View Plumbing Company for the water leak on December 15 in the amount of $975.00. It was:

RESOLVED: That the bill from the Acme Plumbing Company be paid.

Following debate, it was:

RESOLVED: That the contract with the vending machine company for the candy machine in the clubhouse lobby be continued, and the president is authorized to execute the contract. A copy of the contract is to be appended to the minutes.

The social committee report was received and placed on file without objection.

Ms. Smith, chair of a special committee to investigate and report on additional handicapped parking facilities near the clubhouse, presented the committee's report. After debate and amendments, a resolution was adopted as follows:

BACKGROUND: The building official of the Town of Saltonstall, following a complaint from Mrs. Jones of Unit 2B, who has a handicapped son visiting her, checked the parking layout of that cluster and pointed out that the Fair Housing Act and state law require the installation of three additional handicapped parking spaces in that lot, reasonably convenient to the main entrance of the building. The manager submitted a plan showing the conversion of five regular spaces to handicapped spaces at the entrance, and the construction of three new spaces at the south end of the parking lot.

RESOLVED: That the manager contract for the construction of the three additional spaces and the striping and signage of handicapped parking spaces in accordance

continued on next page

continued from previous page

with the standards for such spaces required by the Town of Saltonstall and the plan. The manager should obtain three bids for the work, and submit the lowest responsible bidder's construction contract to the board for approval at the next meeting.

The resolution relating to the use of the game room by nonmembers for parties that was postponed from the last meeting was then taken up. The chair then announced that the invited speaker, Hugh L. Dewey, ESQ. (counsel to the association), would require an earlier departure and should be taken out of order.

Without objection, the motion and appending amendment were laid on the table.

Without objection the agenda was modified to allow Mr. Dewey to speak out of order.

The president then introduced Mr. Hugh Dewey, who spoke about assessment collection and rule enforcement.

Without objection, the resolution relating to the use of the game room by nonmembers was taken from the table. After amendment and further debate the motion was made as follows:

RESOLVED: That the manager would prepare and present to the board at its next meeting a draft contract for the rental of the game room to nonmembers for parties and functions. The manager would present a schedule of charges and extra services that would be provided. The association accountant would be asked to comment and advise the association on the accounting for the income.

Mr. Smith asked for a division of the board by a show of hands. The motion passed by a vote of 5 to 2.

Upon motion made by Mr. Smith it was:

RESOLVED: That the association establish a summer program for teenagers on its lakefront property. Ms. Thomas moved to amend the motion by inserting the words "preteens and" before "teenagers." The amendment passed. The motion to establish the program, with the appending amendment, was referred to a committee of three to be appointed by the chair with instructions to report program details at the next meeting. The chair appointed Mr. Smith, Mr. Dorsey, and Ms. Thomas to the committee.

The meeting adjourned at 10:05 p.m.

_____

Marge Scrivener, Secretary

BY RICHARD LIEVENS, ESQ.

Minutes and Resolutions: The Legal Perspective

Too often, community managers and directors regard board meeting minutes and resolutions as ministerial rather than integral to an association's operation and longevity. These duties must never be taken lightly because maintaining accurate meeting minutes and resolutions has legal significance.

Recording Corporate Acts

The basic purpose of maintaining a minute book is to have a record of corporate acts. Under appropriate circumstances, these records will prove invaluable in upholding a corporate act, evidencing authority, rebutting a presumption of authority, or defending directors.

When an adversary attacks or challenges the validity of a given corporate act, properly kept minutes and resolutions authorizing the act will help verify its validity. Clearly, minutes or resolutions do not, and cannot, create authority where there is none. That is, the applicable statutes, the articles of incorporation, or association bylaws must create the authority; but the minutes and resolutions provide evidence of how the authority was exercised. If no authority exists, no such authority can be exercised.

Minutes and resolutions can also be used to rebut the presumption of authority. For example, it is presumed that the president of a corporation has the authority to perform certain acts. Through proper resolutions recorded in the minutes, other board members may deny such authority—and thus are able to prove, if necessary, that no such authority existed on the president's behalf.

Directors should take great care in ensuring that minutes and resolutions properly reflect voting, abstentions, and objections. This documentation will protect them if a claim of a breach of fiduciary duty is made against them. The minutes can also reflect an individual director's intentions, acts, and omissions, through evidence of voting or dissent. Therefore, it's important for a disagree-

Excerpts from corporation minutes... can be admissible as evidence in most jurisdictions. Some courts have emphasized that minutes of a corporation board meeting are *prima facie* evidence of the facts.

ing board member to ensure that his or her dissention is properly recorded in the minutes.

When a board takes an action outside of the regular course of business, there should be a memorandum or record in the minutes reflecting the board's decision to take the action or refusal to take the action. Again, the purpose is to provide evidence of corporate authority and to defend the board in the event that its action is challenged.

While certain actions, such as decisions to sue and approval of collection procedures, should always be recorded in the minutes, actions that are covered by routine, previously-approved guidelines need not be so specifically stated in the minutes.

It is worth emphasizing that recording a corporate act in the minutes will not validate the act if the board had no such authority. Likewise, failing to record a valid act in the minutes will not necessary render the act invalid. For example, a resolution duly voted on and properly reflected in the minutes for an association to purchase real estate does not make the purchase a valid act if the board lacked such authority. Conversely, if a board exercises its authority to purchase real estate, but through error or omission fails to record the action in the minutes, the corporate act is not necessarily void. It is, however, voidable if the events of the meeting cannot be substantiated in any other way.[1]

Statutory Foundation

Most state laws governing corporations contain specific provisions about taking minutes. Corporations are subject to the applicable Business Corporation Act or Non-Profit Corporation Act of the controlling jurisdiction. Most such laws require corporations to keep minutes of shareholder and director meeting proceedings.[2] Therefore, association boards should analyze applicable statutes to determine minimum minute taking requirements.

Failure to keep contemporaneous minutes as mandated by statute will not necessarily void the corporate act. For example, if the minutes are amended after the fact, this may be sufficient to satisfy statutory requirements.[3] However, if an association refused to repay a loan based on the argument that the promissory note was unenforceable because authorization to obtain the loan was not recorded in the minutes, such an argument would probably fail. A court would likely find that regardless of the statutory obligation to take minutes, if the association received the benefit of the loan, it could not defeat the creditor's claim by merely showing that the transaction was not recorded in the minutes.[4]

In addition to the minimum statutory requirements to keep minutes, the Rules of Evidence (for use in litigation) in most jurisdictions provide that a corporation's records must only be attested by the president and secretary's signature. These documents, accompanied with a corporate seal or certificate, constitute competent evidence in any action or proceeding in which the corporation is involved. Evidence statutes provide associations with an invaluable advantage. When an association is involved in a lawsuit, its minutes or resolutions may, under proper circumstances, be introduced into evidence. Generally, it would not be necessary for witnesses to testify about what happened at the meeting or event.

Under limited circumstances, the court may prohibit witnesses from presenting testimony that would impeach or contradict the minutes.[5] Furthermore, excerpts from corporation minutes, which are maintained according to applicable law and identified by the corporation secretary who recorded the minutes and maintained the minute book, can be admissible as evidence in most jurisdictions. Some courts have emphasized that minutes of a corporation board meeting are *prima facie* evidence of the facts.[6] The minutes will speak for themselves without the need for witnesses or other evidence to prove the acts. This is particularly advantageous for associations if an excessive amount of time has elapsed between the board meeting and court proceeding.

The statutory application of minute taking imposed on profit and nonprofit corporations is the same. Case law decisions from jurisdictions nationwide, however, have differentiated these minute taking standards from those of closely held corporations—corporations that offer no shares for sale and are owned by only a few shareholders who actively conduct the business. Under proper circumstances, the closely held association directors' actions need not be proven by the minutes,[7] but can be proven by oral testamony.[8]

Drafting Meeting Minutes

Meeting minutes should always be drafted during the event and approved by the board within a reasonable time. Occasionally,

Meeting minutes protect board members, uphold and defend corporate acts, evidence authority, and serve as evidence in court cases.

however, minutes are neither drafted nor approved until weeks or months after the meeting. Although this is not advisable, at least one court has held that it is acceptable, noting that subsequent approval of director meeting minutes is a common practice in corporate offices.[9]

Other courts have extended this concept further but have warned against the fabrication of minutes.[10] In the event that mistakes yield incorrect minutes, courts will probably be liberal in allowing the minutes to be corrected in accordance with the truth.[11]

Minutes and resolutions serve definite legal purposes. Meeting minutes protect board members, uphold and defend corporate acts, evidence authority, and serve as evidence in court cases. Community associations, typically organized as nonprofit corporations, are subject to minute taking statutes and requirements. Properly executed minutes and resolutions benefit every corporate entity. Minute taking statutes and requirements serve a protective—not a burdensome—purpose. ∎

References

1. *Cameron and Willacy Counties Community Projects, Inc. et al* v. *Gonzales,* 614 S.W.2d 585 (Tex. Civ. App. Corpus Christi, reh. den. 1981).
2. *Cameron,* Id.
3. *Cameron,* Id.
4. *Scott* v. *Potter Plumbing* 596 S.W.2d 492 (MO Ct. App. So. Dist. 1980).
5. *Emergency Patient Services, Inc.* v. *Crisp,* 602 S.W.2d 26 (MO. Ct. App. Western Dist. 1980).
6. *Acmer* v. *State Transport,* 549 P.2d 1114 no writ.
7. *Kann* v. *Keystone Resources, Inc.,* 575 F. Supp. 1084 (1983).
8. *In re Eastern Erectors, Inc.* 346 F. Supp. 293.
9. *Whitley* v. *Pacific Industries,* Inc., 239 N.E.2d 207.
10. *National Surety Corporation* v. *Crystal Springs Fishing Village,* 326 F. Supp. 1171 (1971).
11. *Hallindale* v. *State,* 326 So.2d 202.

CHAPTER 4

Tape Recording Meetings

BY RAYMOND DIAZ, ESQ., AND LUCIA ANNA TRIGIANI, ESQ.

Boards, Meetings, and Videotape

E very community association needs accurate, permanent minutes. One way to accomplish this is by taping meetings. Taping can create a complete, vivid, and lasting record of not just decisions, but of the discussions leading to decisions. But is taping a good idea?

A condominium in Virginia doesn't think so.

A unit owner filed a lawsuit asking the court to prevent her association from erasing audiotapes of board meetings. She also asked the court to allow her to videotape the meetings. In response, the board explained that it used the audiotapes to help prepare formal, written minutes. Once the minutes are approved, the audiotapes are reused—another meeting is taped over the earlier meeting. Until the audiotape is reused, it is available for review by owners. This, the board asserted, was a reasonable policy that it had the right to make.

At the Board's Discretion

In regard to videotaping, the board claimed that it had the discretion to decide how its meetings would be conducted. Since board members felt videotaping would be disruptive and impede free discussion, they voted not to allow videotaping. The court, the board argued, should not interfere since the association documents placed the decision within the board's discretion.

The owner used Virginia condominium law and the Constitution to support her request for court assistance. But the court agreed with the association. It found that the law allowed the board to adopt a reasonable record retention policy and to run its meetings as it chose, as long as it met statutory requirements.

As this case shows, taping can be troubling because it involves important, competing considerations. On one hand, owners should have access to as much information as possible about the business of their associations. Meeting tapes are an excellent way for owners to review why and how decisions were made. On the other hand, verbatim records can be used to harm an association and, indirectly, the owners' investment.

There are good reasons both for keeping and not keeping audiotapes or videotapes with an association's permanent records. Community associations should consider these benefits and drawbacks before deciding their own policy. It isn't an easy decision. Each association's policy depends on where it strikes the balance among these considerations.

You Oughta Be In Pictures

Perhaps the most obvious reason to tape a meeting is the need for accurate minutes. Like any business, an association needs the formal record of its actions and decisions to be accurate. Statutes confirming the right of owners, contract purchasers, and others to review association records have added force to the need for good records and, therefore, accurate minute taking. If the meeting is taped, minute takers can compare the tape to their notes to double-check accuracy.

Should Boards Tape Meetings?

What are the pros?
- Members can review how decisions were made.
- Tapes help create accurate minutes.
- Minute takers can transcribe minutes without rushing.
- Minute takers can participate in discussions.
- Associations don't need paid staff to take minutes.

What are the cons?
- Tapes can be used as ammunition by opponents.
- More business may be conducted in private, away from cameras.
- Directors may be hesitant to speak when being taped.
- Some directors may grandstand, adding to meeting time.
- Tapes are not always reliable—information may be lost.

Taping...allows members who did not attend a meeting to witness the discussion and decision-making process.

Taping makes minute taking more convenient. It allows the minute taker to transcribe the minutes without rushing to complete them before they forget the details of decisions that were made and written notes fail to refresh the memory. Recording meetings on tape also allows the secretary or other recorder to participate in the meeting more fully.

Because the meeting is taped, the minute taker, who may often be a voting member of the board, is better able to participate in discussions, freed from the preoccupation that complete note-taking requires. Cryptic notes can be fleshed out later by reviewing the meeting tape.

Cost Advantages

For some associations, tape recordings may also save money. Many communities employ minute takers or pay staff members to attend meetings and take minutes. These meeting costs can become a significant budget line item. If the meeting is recorded, the tape may be transcribed and developed into minutes by a staff person or other minute taker who is not paid for attending the meeting.

Taping benefits the members, as well. It allows members who did not attend a meeting to witness the discussion and decision-making process that occurred. Written minutes create a formal record, but they don't convey the full meeting deliberations, replete with inflections and asides. Tapes do.

Lights, Camera—Lawsuit?

Taping meetings can cause problems, however. When meeting tapes are used as evidence, they are frequently introduced against an association. While this is not reason enough to not tape meetings, it is reason to review the arguments against preserving tapes.

An association speaks by its formal resolutions. These resolutions should be complete enough to explain what action is being taken, what authority is relied on to take it, and why the action is taken. Tapes of discussions that led to formal resolutions can serve as ammunition for those who later cast doubt on the motivation or intent of a resolution. It can allow opponents to "rewrite history."

The Camera Never Blinks

In this visual, electronic age, it's easy to see how helpful meeting tapes can be. But they can also cause problems. Consider the following examples:

■ One association videotaped its meetings for later broadcast on closed circuit television. During a debate on a particularly contentious issue, charges, counter-charges, and epithets were hurled between homeowners and directors. As tempers cooled, apologies were extended. Yet months later, a director, having failed in a reelection bid, filed a slander claim against the association and several of its directors. Exhibit number one? The videotape preserved in the association's records.

■ Another board kept audiotapes of its meetings. At one meeting it resolved to accept a vendor's contract on certain conditions. The decision and conditions were part of the written minutes approved by the board. The audiotape of the meeting, though never approved by the board or made an official record, was retained. When a dispute arose after the contract was signed, the vendor used the taped debate to successfully argue that it was never supposed to perform one of the conditions in the written resolution.

Taping meetings may also result in more business being conducted in executive session. Most statutes allow boards to convene in closed session for a number of specific purposes. Frequently, in an effort to allow owners as much information as possible, boards will take up matters in open session. If the board becomes concerned that a verbatim record of their discussions may become available to third parties, however, they may feel obliged to move into closed session. The board may think that it's better to discuss matters in private than to make those discussions available to someone who may use them against the association.

Stage Fright

Another common criticism of taping minutes is that it can restrict discussion and stifle free exchange among the meeting participants. Most associations and their boards can make decisions only in a meeting, unless everyone consents in writing. Discussion, debate, and the free exchange of points of view will frequently lead to the best decision. Many board members, however, are hesitant to speak openly when they are being taped. They become self-

An important element of the records-management plan should be a clear procedure dealing with closed or executive sessions and with minutes of those sessions.

conscious or fear that their words may come back to haunt them or their association. Free discussion leads to better decisions—taping may put that in jeopardy.

In the Virginia lawsuit mentioned previously, one director testified that she was unwilling to mention another association's bad experience with a company during an open meeting—a company the board was about to contract. The reason? She knew the meeting was being taped. Another director testified that he was intimidated by the video camera an owner was running during the meeting. He was afraid that whatever he said might "show up on the six o'clock news."

Playing to the Camera
Not everyone is intimidated by a camera, however. Taping meetings may cause some participants to grandstand. Some people light up when they see the red light on a camera or tape recorder. Brevity goes out the window, histrionics becomes the order of the day, and meetings end in the wee hours. Often, the only means of ensuring brief, business-like meetings is to turn the machines off.

Reliability Issues
The reliability of tapes, especially audiotapes, can also be a problem. Occasionally, important statements are not picked up by the taping machine. Sometimes a tape runs out or breaks unnoticed. If tapes are used as a substitute for written minutes or to augment bare-bones notes, an association may find itself with no record of its actions.

Considerations If You Tape
Each community must reach its own conclusion on whether to tape its meetings. If it does tape, it must decide how long meeting tapes will be kept as part of the association's records. Both of these questions require a review of the pros and cons described above.

Once a policy is established, owners must be aware of it and understand the reasons it was adopted. If the decision is made to tape meetings, that decision is incomplete unless the board also establishes a records-management plan. The records-management plan should address what meetings will be taped, who may tape, the availability of tapes for review and copying, and how long the tapes will be maintained.

An important element of the records-management plan should be a clear procedure dealing with closed or executive sessions and with minutes of those sessions. There is no reason for closed sessions to be taped. Most states allow a board only to *discuss* matters in closed session and requires them to take formal action in open session. Owners can't participate in closed sessions. Thus, even if an association elects to tape its open meetings, it should think long and hard before creating a tape of executive sessions that may, one day, become available to an opponent of the association.

Like good government, community associations conduct their affairs effectively as a series of compromises among important, competing considerations. Successfully striking balances as each compromise is considered is the mark of a successful community. Whether or not to tape association meetings is another issue on which a reflective board must exercise leadership and judgment. The decision that is made should be based on the best interests of the association, not to circumvent owners' rights to information. Any taping should be governed by reasonable restrictions intended to protect association confidences. ∎

BY HENRY GOODMAN, ESQ.

Tape Recording Meetings

Recently, when a dissident group of owners in a Massachusetts condominium claimed the board meeting minutes did not accurately reflect their views, the board announced it would begin taping meetings. The goal was to create more accurate minutes. But the dissidents then alleged it was illegal to tape their comments without their permission, and that doing so showed a lack of respect. They refused to grant permission. The board, although it believed that taping was legal, destroyed the tape out of respect for the dissidents.

As the association's attorney, it seemed strange to me that the board showed such respect for a group that intends to unseat it. A group so concerned that its arguments lack substance that it does not want its words preserved on tape. Nonetheless, this case raises legitimate issues about recording. Can comments at a meeting be legally taped and used when a speaker states that he or she objects to the taping, and refuses to allow the board to press the record button?

Key Word: Secret

In some states, privacy and wiretapping laws grant every individual the right to prevent his or her conversations or messages from being recorded or intercepted. In fact, such laws make such interception (including tape recording) a crime. In these statutes the term "interception" means to secretly hear, secretly record—or aid another in doing so —the contents of any wire or oral communication.

The key word is "secretly." If the board announces at the beginning of the meeting—and every time a person enters—that the meeting is being recorded, the recording is not a secret. Therefore, the board can legally tape record the meeting if it follows that formula. Thus, it is legal to record the minutes of a meeting, despite objections, so long as the recording is not a secret. Secret recordings can be a crime with severe penalties.

In Massachusetts, for example, secret taping is considered illegal wiretapping. In some state statutes, taping is illegal only if the spoken word is in a private forum, not a public forum. An open board meeting would likely constitute an open forum.

Those Who Object

Community association attorneys often disagree about the benefits of taping. In my opinion, taping is desirable. It helps the secretary or clerk prepare the written minutes accurately. Although it isn't necessary to quote each speaker verbatim, it allows the secretary to quote important phraseology. If disputes erupt, the association can save recordings to determine what was actually said at the meeting.

What about the people who object? They still have a right to not be recorded. They can leave the meeting or remain and not speak. If they do speak, their words may be recorded and, if applicable, used against them. Their mere objection is insufficient.

On occasion someone with something important to say will refuse to say it into a tape recorder. There's a danger in permitting unrecorded communication—the individual may later deny actually making such statements, rendering it worthless.

Nonetheless, the board may occasionally need to hear such comments. But what if the speaker is intimidated? Sometimes speakers want nothing that proves they're making accusations against another owner. They may not want to be on tape suggesting something unpopular. Yet the board may consider such information to be crucial. In an appropriate situation, the board could vote to suspend taping. However, the minutes should still show that the board responded to the information imparted by the speaker. In my opinion, the minutes should reflect more than the board's ultimate decision. It should show the information upon which the board based its actions.

Are there options available when residents refuse to be taped or to have a record made of their comments? Of course. In my opinion, however, this is weak information. For example, a person may secretly give information to a board member who is supposed to impart it to the board. The board member may be sworn to secrecy as to the speaker's identity. But the alleged facts would amount to hearsay. If there is a conflict, the board cannot rely on such unsubstantiated third-hand information in court.

The mere knowledge that the tape is rolling may cause board members to think about their positions and make more rational decisions.

Members Taping Meetings

Sometimes homeowners either openly or secretly tape board meetings without the board's permission. And once directors learn a homeowner is recording their discussions and decisions, they usually question whether they must allow the taping to continue.

I would argue that the board's statements and actions during an open meeting are public in nature and, therefore, are not susceptible to privacy protections.

When the board has a legitimate interest in keeping its actions private, it may retire to executive session. Issues that a board may discuss during executive session include:

■ Potentially defamatory matters, such as complaints of criminal activity.

■ Matters in which an owner may have a right to privacy, such as financial issues.

■ Privileged matters, such as attorney/client advice or litigation strategy.

Meetings held to discuss these issues are not open to the public. All private conversations are subject to the prohibition of secret taping. If the taping is open and obvious, the board may eject the individual recording the meeting.

A Double-Edged Sword

Some lawyers disagree with taping entirely. One of my partners believes that taping meeting minutes is a bad idea. He feels that minutes should memorialize decisions—not what was said. However, he agrees that divergent votes should be recorded. He also believes recording can be stifling. The person with information may be afraid to have his words on tape. Ultimately, he claims, taping has no practical use and can come back to "bite the board."

In that regard, taping can be a double-edged sword. The tape—and the statements contained on the tape—could be used not only against a speaker, but also against the board. This is especially true if the owner is speaking on behalf of the board or if the board acts wrongly.

This doesn't mean speakers should fear taping. Most minutes simply record the gist of a speaker's comments. Taping is more accurate. A speaker's comments are less likely to be mischaracterized. In fact, the mere knowledge that the tape is rolling may cause board members to think about their positions and make more rational decisions.

Storing Tapes

If the board is to tape, it should establish a policy on how long to keep tapes before destroying them. Generally, I recommend keeping tapes for at least a year. Tapes containing controversial matters can be kept longer.

One additional word of advice: do not tape executive sessions where you are discussing personalities, legal strategies, or matters covered by privacy rights. Such information can fall into the wrong hands and the board could be sued. The board could also lose its claim that the issues are privileged information.

Although minutes need not be verbatim transcripts, they should accurately reflect the speaker's position. They should also reflect the board's ultimate decision. If a decision is wrong and the board is sued, dissenters may be saved from liability—they can show they did not go along with the decision. It is also helpful politically, in the next election, to be able to show the voting positions of each of the incumbents running for re-election, as well as the attitude and position of a board member who is being recalled. ∎

BY MJ KEATTS

California Association Televises Board Meetings

When board meetings at Canyon Lakes Property Association convene, the cameras roll. The California association began broadcasting board meetings on the community's cable system to restore meeting order and increase accessibility, said former Canyon Lake manager Bill Hallman, CMCA, PCAM. Prior to televising the meetings, dissension among members sometimes turned into violent quarrels.

Rolling the camera is one way associations can retain meeting order. Televising board meetings worked for Canyon Lakes, but not without a few drawbacks.

While out-of-control meetings are a thing of the past for Canyon Lakes, so are large owner turnouts. Unless a hot item, such as a fee increase, is on the agenda, about 10 of the association's 13,000 residents usually attend each board meeting.

"A good number of the residents watch the meetings on television," Hallman said. "Some residents show up at the end of the meeting to make a statement."

Residents who watch the meeting on television only see the second half of the show. Because board members discuss agenda items during a pre-meeting work session, which isn't televised, they usually don't debate during the board meeting. Only homeowners who attend the work session will know board members' positions.

"Being on television limits board members' ability to discuss the issues," Hallman said. "When there are cameras in the room, you're aware of what you're saying." Although the board members may be camera shy, Hallman doesn't hesitate to take advantage of a televised board meeting. He frequently makes news announcements during a televised meeting. ∎

CHAPTER 5

Executive Sessions

BY KENNETH BUDD

Behind Closed Doors

Most community associations realize the importance of holding open board meetings. There are times, however, when a board needs to meet in closed executive sessions.

So when can this happen? When can a board meet behind closed doors? The answer may lie in your state's condominium or homeowner association laws. Some states, such as Florida, require all board meetings to be open. In Virginia, boards are required to vote before entering executive session. Other state statutes specifically list the topics that can be discussed in executive sessions.

In general, most experts consider pending litigation, personnel issues, and contract negotiations to be appropriate for closed meetings.

Pending litigation would include any action taken by the association, from construction defect suits to actions against covenant violators. It also could include meetings with the association attorney. Personnel issues could include employee issues, such as harassment suits and job performance.

"Executive sessions are good for personal issues," said Ellen Hirsch de Haan, an attorney with Becker & Poliakoff in St. Petersburg, Florida. "It could be discussions of employee issues or a conversation with a homeowner regarding collection problems."

The key is that discussions of community association business issues should be open to all members. Executive session, if allowed by state law, is a privilege that should not be abused.

Information is Confidential

Should executive sessions be announced in advance to the membership? Most experts say "yes." Members should be informed of any items on the agenda that will be discussed in executive session. That way, they're less likely to be offended when asked to leave a meeting.

"The more openly you communicate, the more you can avoid claims that the board is sneaky," Hirsch de Haan said.

Vote in Open Session

Even though the meeting may be closed, resulting motions must be voted in open session, and the results should be recorded in the minutes. If appropriate, communicate the results of a closed meeting, but remember: the information discussed in an executive session is confidential. While the association may publish that the board met in a closed session to discuss an unresolved architectural violation, it should not reveal the member's name or the details of the meeting.

"Executive sessions are generally considered confidential meetings and they should be viewed as such," said Virginia attorney Ken Chadwick. "If a board member discusses something with a friend that should be confidential, that could lead to trouble."

Chadwick worked with an association that nearly lost its directors' and officers' insurance coverage when confidential information was leaked. The board had split into factions. A member of one faction sued the association. It soon became evident that information discussed in executive session was going to the other side.

This was considered a breach of fiduciary duty, which put the association's directors and officers insurance at risk. Since the board was not cooperating with the prosecution of the case, the insurance carrier said it could no longer defend the association. As a result, Chadwick told the directors that they could be personally liable if they refused to keep information confidential.

Closed or Secret?

Though executive sessions are sometimes necessary, boards must be careful not to abuse the privilege. Closed meetings should not be used simply because the board wants to discuss a potentially unpopular subject or avoid confrontation with members.

"It's a tool that needs to be used in certain circumstances, but should not be misused," Chadwick said. "Most associations are careful—they understand that it can appear improper."

Boards may think of executive sessions as closed meetings, but members may see them as secret meetings. Boards should avoid that perception by limiting the number of executive sessions they hold, announcing the sessions they do hold, and explaining the reasons for the sessions. ∎

BY CHRISTOPHER DURSO

Open and Shut Meetings

If your board is meeting behind closed doors, you must have something to hide. Avoiding that perception—and avoiding lawsuits, too—means being as open about your business as you can.

When can (and should) you clamp down? What can you keep private, and what can you leave open to the public? That depends on what your governing documents say, what type of association you have, and what state you live in. Needless to say, when in doubt, you should check with a lawyer.

Beth Mulcahy, an attorney with the Mulcahy Law Firm, PC, in Phoenix, Arizona, says that she gets questions about open meetings every week. "There are always problems that come up," Mulcahy says, "but almost all of them can be solved by looking at the language of the statutes and following it."

On the surface, board meetings seem like a no-brainer. Association residents are invited, and everything transpires out in the open. Except it doesn't usually happen exactly like that.

Rather, each state has its own approach. Some have passed "sunshine" laws and other legislation governing the operation of condominiums and homeowner associations. The Arizona Open Meeting Law, for example, requires that notice of a board meeting be given 48 hours in advance and that the meeting be open to all association members. Closed-door executive sessions are allowed—but, according to Mulcahy, only to discuss personnel, legal advice, litigation, or rules enforcement.

Florida has similar association-specific provisions. Its Condominium Act, Cooperative Act, and Homeowners Association Act all guarantee homeowners the right to attend board and committee meetings, though only the condominium and cooperative laws give them the right to speak at those meetings.

Other states don't spell everything out to the degree that Arizona and Florida do. According to Lynn Boyet, CMCA, AMS, of EMB Management Inc., in Bellevue, Washington, her state's laws "allow the individual association articles of incorporation and bylaws to dictate their meeting practices and criteria. The laws do not require open board meetings." Boyet adds: "In my experience, the practice of holding private or public board meetings varies with each association and seems to relate to the size of the community and its form of management." In small associations, she says, it's difficult to get homeowners to serve on the board and to achieve a quorum, so "unannounced board meetings are often called to act on pending issues that need resolution."

By the Light of Day

Regardless of what state laws or your governing documents require, many residents subscribe to the belief that the light of day is the best disinfectant—as do many professionals. The idea is that decisions affecting the community should be made before the community. "What do we do in homeowner associations that's worth being so secret?" C.J. Klug asks. "Of course, I'm a big believer that there are no secrets....When more than two people know something, eventually it will come out."

Or your efforts to hide will only draw more attention. "I had one board that I felt went into executive session simply to avoid conflict with homeowners via the discussion," says Denise Bower, CMCA, AMS, PCAM, of Community Management Inc., in Portland, Oregon. "And I think they've had more problems with homeowners saying, 'Wait a minute, we want to know why you're going into executive session.'"

Some Tips

Announce meetings and post agendas. John Davey, CMCA, AMS, PCAM, president of Comet Management, in northern New Jersey, mails out a meeting schedule in advance for the entire coming year. Says Davey: "Some meetings are canceled due to lack of a quorum of the board, but there are no unannounced meetings." Posting an agenda closer to the meeting date will keep residents that much more in the loop.

Explain executive sessions. Knowing what you can't talk about

It's not a good idea to permit your owners to comment on business while you're conducting it.

is as important as knowing what you can. Be familiar with the issues that you're required to keep confidential, and be able to explain to curious or suspicious residents why you're meeting in executive session.

Allow for homeowner input. It's not a good idea to permit your owners to comment on business while you're conducting it. But consider setting aside some time at the beginning or end of a meeting for public input, to let owners know that you're interested in what they have to say.

Anticipate. Before he got into community associations, C.J. Klug was a city manager for 20 years, and he brought with him some of the techniques of government—which tends to assume openness as a default position. For example, Nellie Gail Ranch not only advertises the meeting at which its budget will be voted on but announces that a copy is in the office for anyone to review. "That wasn't in our CC&Rs," Klug says, "but that's a common way cities do it."

No one ever comes in to look at the budget, but, according to Klug, that's not important. "The more you do in advance," he says, "the less you're likely to build up the negativism that leads to people challenging everything." ∎